PAYING WITHOUT MONEY

MONEY POWER

Jason Cooper

Rourke

Publishing LLC

Vero Beach, Florida 32964

www.rourkepublishing.com

PHOTO CREDITS: © Armentrout; © Corel Corporation; © East Coast Studios; © Evon Thornton; © Oscar C. Williams

Cover Photo: *Credit cards, checks, and debit cards are ways of paying without using money.*

Editor: Frank Sloan

Cover design by Nicola Stratford

Library of Congress Cataloging-in-Publication Data

Cooper, Jason
   Paying without money / Jason Cooper
     p. cm. — (Money power)
   Includes bibliographical references and index.
   Summary: Explains how people can use checking accounts, debit and credit cards, travelers' checks, and electronic funds transfers to pay for goods and services.
   ISBN 1-58952-213-3
   1. Money—Juvenile literature. 2. Checks—Juvenile literature. 3. Credit cards—Juvenile literature. 4. Debit cards—Juvenile literature. 5. Travelers' checks—Juvenile literature. 6. Electronics funds transfers—Juvenile literature. [1. Money 2. Finance, Personal.] I. Title.

HG221.5 .C666 2002
332.1'78—dc21
                                        2001048908

Printed in the USA

CG/CG

TABLE OF CONTENTS

PAYING WITHOUT MONEY

People use money to buy things or services. Sometimes they pay for those things or services with cash—coins and paper **bills**. But many people make purchases without using cash.

People without cash may trade goods or services for other goods and services. Most people today who don't want to pay in cash use checks, credit cards, and **electronics**.

BANKS AND MONEY

People can make purchases without using cash because of banks. Banks help people move money from person to person or business to business without handling cash.

Banks are businesses that take care of money. Banks hold money. Banks loan money. Banks **transfer**, or move, money from place to place.

Banks keep money safely for people in what are called **accounts**. An account is a person's own special pool of money.

Banks offer information and services for saving and investing money.

SAVINGS A?E

INVESTMENT
A

ESTMENT
IONS

SAVIN PLAN

Deposit

		Dollars	Cents
Cash		75	00
		150	00
List Checks		28	00
		479	68
Total			7.3
Less Cash Back			
Net Deposit			

HUGHES   Date: Sep 7th

BEACON ST. BOSTON

RT

The Code # Is:

To Your.
OW/MM Checking 51   60   65   80   90
Savings

50

50   3

3   C 22108

B 609

2

5

5

DEPOSIT/PAYMENT EN

PAYMENT ENVELOPE   DEPOSIT/

ENVELOPE   DEPOSIT/PAYMENT EN

DEPOSIT

CHECKING ACCOUNTS

Many people have checking accounts. Checks allow people to make purchases without having to pay with cash.

To use a check, a person has to put money into his or her checking account at a bank. That account has its own number to separate it from every other checking account. If someone puts $100 in a checking account, that person can write checks that total up to $100.

A signed check allows a bank to release money from your account.

New England Telephone

EX Company

CREDIT LINE $5,000

CASH OR CREDIT AVAILABLE $4,042.25

JULY 1993 STAT...

MIDDLESEX-ESSEX. MA
P.M
MAR 27
1993

LIEF CENTER
WLER
R ST.
01960

CLOSING DATE 07/16/93

DAYS IN CYCLE

MINIMUM PAYMENT DUE $.00

PAYMENT D... 08/1...

CHARGES

CREDITS

PHONE ORDER

PHONE ORDER

36.49
29.98
96.49
325.

BROOKLYN PAR
WATERTOWN
BROOKLYN PAR
ERETT
LAX

MA
RNDTRP
MA
RNDTRP

NEW ENGLAND

A check is a piece of paper printed with the name of the user and the bank. It is worthless until the user fills in the blank lines on the check and signs the check.

Many people pay their bills and make purchases with checks. The bank takes money from the check writer's account to pay the person who receives the check.

When you pay a bill by check, you must keep a record of the amount paid.

*You need a credit or debit card to get money from
an ATM (automated teller machine).*

Instead of using money, this woman trades the dolls she has made for food and clothing.

DEBIT CARDS

Debit cards work much like checks. Banks offer debit cards to people with checking accounts. The account holder presents the debit card to pay for a purchase. The purchase price is taken from the card holder's checking account at the bank.

Many people like debit cards because this means they don't have to write checks for things they buy.

At many gas stations you can use credit and debit cards.

Use any of these cards.

TURN OFF ENGINE   NO SMOKING

CREDIT-INSERT CARD

PAYMENT KEYS

INSERT
CARD
FULLY

REMOVE
QUICKLY

CREDIT CARDS

Many people buy things and they don't use cash or checks. Instead, they buy "on **credit**." If a person has a good record of paying his or her bills or debts, he or she may be able to buy "on credit." That means a person promises to pay in the future for something he or she buys now.

A loan from a bank to buy a house is a kind of credit.

A common way of buying on credit is the use of a credit card. A credit card user presents a small, plastic credit card to a store for payment of a purchase. The credit card company pays the business for the amount of the purchase. Then the credit card company sends a monthly bill to the card user.

A credit card user is actually borrowing money to pay for purchases. Credit card companies charge **interest** on the money they lend. Interest is money charged for the use of someone else's money.

TRAVELERS' CHECKS

Travelers' checks offer another way people can pay for purchases without using cash. Travelers' checks can be bought from banks. They can be used worldwide in place of cash. If travelers' checks are lost or stolen, they will be replaced.

Many people who travel overseas or who might otherwise carry large amounts of cash like travelers' checks.

A $20 travelers' check has the same value as a $20 bill.

ELECTRONIC MONEY

Many people and businesses today transfer money electronically. Electronic transfers take place through electric wires or computers.

Some banks, for example, allow their customers to pay bills electronically. The customer moves money from one account to another by using buttons on a telephone or computer key pad. Many businesses both collect and pay bills electronically.

People will use even more electronic movement of money in the future.

GLOSSARY

accounts (uh KOWNTS) — personal deposits of money in your name in a bank

bills (BILLZ) — pieces of paper money, such as a dollar bill

credit (KREHD it) — the amount of money that one can borrow

electronics (EE lek TRON icks) — electric systems that process exchanges of money

interest (IN trest) — the charge for borrowing money

transfer (TRANZ fur) — to move from one place to another

INDEX

Further Reading

Otfinoski, Steve. *The Kids' Guide to Money: Earning It, Saving It, Spending It, Growing It, Sharing It*. Scholastic, 1996

Websites To Visit

http://www.treas.gov/opc/
http://www.frbsf.org/currency/index.html
http://www.moneyfactory.com

About The Author

Jason Cooper has written several children's books about a variety of topics for Rourke Publishing, including recent series *China Discovery* and *American Landmarks*. Cooper travels widely to gather information for his books. Two of his favorite travel destinations are Alaska and the Far East.